ENGLISH COSTUME OF
THE NINETEENTH CENTURY

1836

English Costume

of the

Nineteenth Century

Drawn and described by

IRIS BROOKE

Adam and Charles Black

FIRST PUBLISHED 1929
REPRINTED 1935, 1947, 1950, 1958, 1970, 1977
A. & C. BLACK LTD
35 BEDFORD ROW, LONDON WC1R 4JH
© A. & C. BLACK LTD

ISBN 0 7136 0159 0

PRINTED IN GREAT BRITAIN BY TINDAL PRESS LTD.

FOREWORD

IT was in the Nineteenth Century that the Modern World took shape, and it would be strange indeed if the political and economic revolutions which determined the history of Europe during that hundred years should have found no reflection in the evolution of our clothes. In their hatred of the embroidered garments of the nobility, the men and women of 1789 turned, on the one hand, to English country fashions, and, on the other, to what they imagined was the clothing of the Ancient Greeks. The result was that top-boots for men and a single, flimsy, chemise-like garb for women became the accepted wear. Men abandoned knee-breeches, long flapped surcoats and wigs ; women gave up loops, brocade and the use of powder on the hair. But the greatest revolution of all was that henceforth the classes could no longer be distinguished by striking differences of dress. Yet changes in fashion, especially for women, happened all the more frequently, for only by adopting the very latest novelty could the woman of wealth distinguish herself from her sisters. For a whole century the accepted forms of male and female costume had remained fundamentally the same. Once the tradition was broken, anything might have happened. What actually did happen, and how we arrived by easy stages at something approaching the dress of to-day, it is the purpose of the following pages to show.

J. L.

1800

IN the time of the French Directory, during the first flush of freedom from the old eighteenth-century modes, women's dress had pushed daring to the point of indecency, and men's, with its immense tails and prodigious neckcloth, had been more fantastic than the style it had superseded. But by 1800 sobriety had won its victory. Feminine dress was still in one piece, divided into skirt and bodice by a cord or ribbon tied immediately under the breasts. A short jacket was sometimes added as a protection against the cold—a protection much needed, as the garments of the day were scantier even than those of modern times.

The materials used were excessively light muslin, batiste, lawn—and the caricaturists made merry over the disasters of revelation consequent upon the slightest sudden shower. Gérard's painting of Psyche set a fashion for white dresses which was very generally followed. The wild hair of 1794 had been drawn closer to the head, but it was still short both for men and women. Men's coats had assumed the cut-away shape which persists to-day in formal evening and morning dress. Their neckcloths had shrunk to moderate proportions and the beginnings of the modern bow-tie were apparent. Breeches had not yet been entirely abandoned, but were already on their last legs. The three-cornered hat with plumes had disappeared, and the ancestor of the silk-hat was already taking shape.

1800—1805

SOON after the beginning of the century, women began to be bored with the single garment, and to wear over it a second, cut open in front or short in the form of a tunic. The romantic elements of the late eighteenth century began to break through the pseudo-classical crust, and dressmakers began to puff the sleeves in the manner of the Tudor period and to encircle the neck with the beginnings of a high lace frill. Already in 1801, ruffs made of Brabant lace, and called "Betsies," after Queen Elizabeth, had made their appearance, and although the high waist continued, revolutionary simplicity was gone for ever. The poke-bonnet, which was afterwards to attain to such formidable dimensions, had been known as early as 1797, and by 1805 had begun to be common.

Men's hats, in that warlike age, were sometimes cocked in the military or naval fashion, but the high-crowned beaver was already winning its way to universal acceptance. In masculine clothes the ascendancy of Brummel was establishing the reputation of English tailors for fineness of cut which has persisted until to-day. An ideal of cleanliness was adopted both of the clothes and of the person, which is one of the debts which the modern world owes to the early nineteenth-century dandy.

1805—1810

AFTER 1805 the new style may be said to have become
established. The dress fitted closely, but no longer
trailed on the ground as before. The train of the early years
of the century was abolished, and the skirt began to be
worn shorter. By 1808, in some garments at least, the
feet were free, and two years later ankles were visible. The
shawl had made its first appearance in England as long ago
as 1786, but it became the rage during the first ten years of
the new century. The passion for " draperies " encouraged
the use of shawls, and cashmere became extremely fashionable. Even the introduction of fur cloaks from Vienna
about 1808 failed to displace the shawl, and it continued to
be worn until quite late in the century. Nothing in women's
dress, however, was of such importance as what was hap-
pening to men's—the triumph of trousers. Originally the
costume of the English sailor or the French *sans-culotte*, they
gradually made their way into the most fashionable society.
Soon only elderly men were to be seen wearing breeches,
and after Waterloo they may be said to have disappeared
from ordinary attire.

1800—1810

THE first ten years of the century witnessed, as we have seen, the beginning of the poke-bonnet, and the development of men's linen and neckcloths along the lines they have followed ever since. The frilled shirt, allowed to project through a very low-cut waistcoat, became the ancestor of the modern evening-dress shirt, and it is curious to note that the soft shirt with many pleats, which made its appearance after the European War, was in reality less of a novelty than a revival.

Hair, which about 1798 had begun to be cut quite short, was, in the early years of the new century, brushed forward over the eyes. By 1809 it was the fashion to curl it, and shortly afterwards was adopted the plain short cut which has existed, with minor modifications, ever since. Women's hair began to be worn longer.

1810

THE general dress of the day was plainer, both for men and women, than it had been for centuries, but ceremonial dress was still worn at the English Court, and Napoleon re-introduced it into his own. Indeed, in spite of the war against England, the winter of 1809-10, just before Napoleon's second marriage, was the most brilliant and extravagant season of any that had been seen since the fall of the *ancien régime*. Men's fashions had firmly adopted the English mode, but women's continued to be inspired by Paris. The turban, which is said to have been inspired by the campaigns in Egypt, had become a recognised item of feminine attire. Stays came in during the winter of 1809 and persisted for a century.

1810-1815

EVEN in winter, morning dresses continued to be made of muslin, although bombazine (then considered a very elegant material) was also worn. Dinner dresses were made of velvet and satin. Velvet frocks trimmed with swansdown were popular about 1812. Collars, for day wear, became noticeably higher, and short sleeves disappeared. In the evening, gowns were cut square over the bosom and very low. Shoulder straps entirely disappeared. Dresses were trimmed with frills or rolls of the same material, and it was not until 1812 that different coloured trimmings began to be used. The article of attire most characteristic of the period was the pelisse, a kind of over-dress, buttoning down the front, and sometimes made fairly short in order to show nine or ten inches of a white muslin dress underneath. In very severe weather a " pilgrim's cloak " was thrown over the pelisse. Furs also were worn in cold weather, and ankle-boots for women made their appearance. They were almost heelless, but still pointed, and sometimes laced behind. Slippers had slashings of contrasting colours. Gold ornaments began to replace the coloured stones which had previously been popular.

In men's dress, trousers are seen to have won their triumph, and the astonishing reign of the tall hat has been successfully inaugurated. Some older features of dress, however, still persisted, notably the coat with many overlapping capes, which survived among coachmen even later. Waistcoats once more came down to the hips.

1815-1820

THE beginning of the long peace marked a considerable change in the general shape of women's dresses. The waist became even shorter than it had been before, and the skirt descended from it in straight lines to just above the ankles. The bottom of the skirt, however, was very much wider and much more decorated, generally with somewhat stiff *rouleaux* of material—a kind of incipient (and external) crinoline. The use of transparent materials worn over opaque ones began to be appreciated, and it became fashionable to wear a frock of pink crape over a slip of white satin, or a dress of net (the name " patent net " shows how recently it had been invented) over a slip of coloured satin or sarsnet. Sleeves became very elaborate, and the exaggeration of the shoulders foreshadowed the fashions of the 'thirties. Puckered muslin was used to give to sleeves the puffed appearance of the time of Henry VIII, and the Tudor ruff round the neck emphasized the period from which dressmakers were drawing their inspiration. The influence of Scott was also to be seen in the fashion for plaid scarves and sashes, which were very popular about 1817.

Men's fashions exhibited no change worth recording.

1810-1820

THE military enthusiasms of the time are seen in the adoption for women's dress of details from soldiers' uniforms. Even the forms of headgear were copied, and froggings and epaulettes gave an added touch of patriotic fantasy. The so-called Wellington hat, the Wellington bonnet, and even the Wellington jacket (made of twilled sarsnet and worn for dinner parties) were extremely popular. There was also a Wellington mantle, like a small Spanish cloak, and it is sad to think that the name of the great soldier, having rested lightly for a moment on so many articles of attire, should, in the end, have clung only to boots.

What was known as the plain cottage bonnet became somewhat more elaborate, being cut out in front so as to display a lace cap underneath. Hats became higher and were decorated with flowers, feathers, or bands of plaited " grogram " or puffed gauze. At this period, and much later, hats were worn in the evening with everything but full dress, for which flowers or feathers were substituted.

Ostrich plumes became fashionable, and, worn upright in the hair, they have persisted for court dress until to-day.

Men's collars continued to be high, and the neck-cloth was still voluminous.

1820

ALTHOUGH white was still fashionable, coloured dresses were sometimes worn, and, as a somewhat daring innovation, a coloured bodice with a white skirt. The waistband, which was occasionally coloured even when the dress was white, sank to its normal position immediately above the hips. Sleeves continued to be puffed and slashed in a pseudo-Elizabethan style. The hat was large, and plumes, sometimes of various colours, were much worn.

Drawers, long, tight-fitting, and trimmed with lace, began to be worn by women, although they were not universal until the 'thirties, or later. Little girls also wore them long, so that they protruded several inches below the skirts, and, had they not been so elaborate, would have looked like trousers. Sometimes these " pantalettes " were false, being merely attached by tapes above the knee.

Trousers for men were by this time almost universal, their supremacy never to be disputed until the coming of knickerbockers at the very end of the century. The tall hat was broad-brimmed, with the crown wider at the top than at the bottom. The collar of the shirt rose almost to the sides of the mouth, and the front of the shirt was frilled and allowed to protrude through the waistcoat.

1820-1825

LITTLE change was seen in women's dress during the early 'twenties. The waist remained high and bodices, which were very short, had a *bouffant* drapery over the bust, sometimes made of silk netting, to give (in the words of a contemporary chronicle) a fullness where nature had been less prodigal. Ball dresses were short, and the padded *rouleau* at the bottom gave them that weighted appearance so typical of the period. They were made of striped crape, flock gauze, rainbow gauze, plain *barège*, silk or tulle. Colours were tender rather than violent, the favourites being lavender grey, pale yellow, mignonette-green, and rose. Scarlet ball dresses were, however, not unknown. Hats were large and elaborate, being lined with velvet and trimmed with large plumes. There was a passion for feathers, and they were considered essential even on " satin bonnets for the morning lounge." Trimmings were sometimes of polished steel. Turbans of figured gauze were the favourite head-dresses of married ladies of middle age. For evening wear they were adorned with a few pearls or, in mourning, with a bandeau of jet or bugles, and a plume of feathers. Young ladies wore wreaths of flowers made of crape.

For men, the fit of clothes became even more important than it had previously been. The tails of a dress-coat were now cut out separately and sewn onto the body of the coat, so that the latter followed the figure more closely. Hips and chest were exaggerated by padding. Trousers either ended well above the ankles or were cut long enough to be strapped under the boots.

1825-1830

ALREADY, by 1827, the sleeves of gowns had begun to assume the swollen appearance so typical of the next decade. In ball dresses they looked like enormous epaulettes, which indeed was the name given to them. Skirts were growing wider, and the turned-down white collars larger, the Vandyke succeeding the Elizabethan. Hats were rounder and perched more on the top of the head. They were sometimes made of fine straw and worn over a small lace cap. Very long ribbons of the same colours as the trimming of the hat floated over the shoulders.

Chintzes came into favour for morning dresses, and for home costume during the day. Cambric skirts were bordered with shawl material, and a reticule of the same stuff was carried in the hand.

The corsage was longer in the waist than it had been, and the pleats of the skirt were gathered into the band, giving an equal fullness all round. This was known as the Dutch fashion, and did not last very long. Waists were very tight. Shawls of red cashmere were much worn as an outdoor covering.

1820-1830

TO the modern eye there is something very astonishing in the apparent unwillingness of women of the 'twenties ever to have their heads completely uncovered. The minimum for morning wear was an elaborate lace cap, and for evening, a towering wreath or some large ornament of metal. Very big hats with plumes were worn for dinner parties, and even at the opera—it is to be hoped, only by those who sat in boxes. Even so, a hat as broad as the lady's shoulders adorned with half-a-dozen immense ostrich feathers cannot have added much to the enjoyment of the attendant gallant.

Hair was sometimes parted on the forehead à *la Madonna*, with ringlets over each temple descending nearly as low as the tip of the ear. Sprigs of flowers were scattered among the bows in the hair, such bows being of coloured gauze ribbon striped with silver. Very high ornamental tortoiseshell combs were not known towards the end of the decade. They sustained two large curls, known as the Apollo's knot. Ball dresses were cut fairly low in a boat shape, and were very elaborately trimmed at the edge of the corsage.

1830

THE distinguishing feature of women's dress in the 'thirties was its enormous breadth caused by the width of the skirt and the extreme fullness of the sleeves. Skirts were short, and this exaggerated the squat impression of the whole costume. The sleeves were so voluminous, even in evening-dress, that they had to be kept extended by wicker frames or even by small feather cushions.

Hair-dressing was very elaborate, the hair being built up from the head and crowned with flowers, feathers, or jewelled combs. During the mourning for George IV, black and white crape flowers were used to decorate the hair in full dress.

Leghorn, rice straw, and *gros de Naples* were the materials most in favour for promenade hats, the brims of which were very wide, and cut so as to conceal as little of the face as possible. They were trimmed with dahlias, anemones, and field-flowers, sometimes mingled with ears of corn.

Full dress tended to be fairly simple, muslin being most usual ; and, when mourning was over, this was generally white. If coloured, dresses were of one colour only, the favourites being rose, blue, or lilac.

1830-1835

IN the early 'thirties corsages were tight at the waist and long, the heart-shaped bodice being the most popular. Velvet was very much worn, even in combination with silk. Crape, and a material called "blond," were also used, and it was possible to have a dress *à la Taglioni* of tulle worked in lamy. Printed satins were much in use for scarfs and shawls. Poplin dresses were trimmed with satin bows. Quite young women at balls or parties wore brocaded gauze dresses of pink or white, or white organdie dresses, with a rose in the hair and a rose at the girdle. Fashionable colours of the early 'thirties were pink, blue, "grenat," *violet de Parme*, and lapis-lazuli; but yellow was a favourite colour for ball dresses.

Shoes were flat-heeled and square-toed, and for evening wear were generally of black satin. Silk stockings were very fine and transparent, but it was the custom to wear another pair underneath, of flesh-coloured cashmere.

The so-called Grecian coiffure was very fashionable, but hair was also worn in plain bands or with ringlets wide apart on the temples and descending low on the cheeks.

1835-1840

THE place of the fichu was taken by various kinds of collar, generally worn low and turned back. Collars could be made of plain velvet or of watered silk embroidered in colour. Tight sleeves or sleeves enlarging just above the elbow (known as sleeves *à la jardinière*) took the place of the exaggerated sleeves of the early part of the decade. Skirts became considerably longer, and, as their weight was becoming oppressive, Paris dressmakers, in 1839, introduced a modified form of hoop which could be added to or disengaged from the corset at pleasure. However, the *crino zephir* (or horse-hair tissue under petticoats) was still worn.

Shawls were worn even in summer, when they were made of muslin, lace, or net. Plain cashmere shawls with deep fringes were also fashionable.

Children's dresses were mostly made of muslin or cambric with lace insertion.

There was considerable elaboration of such details of the toilette as handkerchiefs. These were sometimes embroidered in red, blue, or brown, with the name of the owner in Gothic characters, surmounted by her coat-of-arms. Black silk mittens were extremely common.

1830-1840

DURING the early thirties curls were much worn, and
sometimes these were supported by wire frames
and ornamental combs.

Towards the end of the decade the coiffure became very
much lower, and many women, especially among the young,
wore twists of hair falling on the neck, fastened with Italian
pins. Long ringlets made their appearance, and sometimes
the hair falling on the cheek was twisted spirally and the
ends placed behind the ears.

The poke-bonnet was almost universal, but an attempt
was made to raise it from the face by pulling down the brim
at the sides. Then the crown was lowered, and at the end
of the decade the whole hat was much smaller, although the
peak was still fairly high. Straw hats became very general
towards 1840. They were trimmed with crape or gauze of
the same colour as the hat, or with field-flowers placed very
far back on the brim. About 1839 an extraordinary substitute
for the cap was introduced. This was the " arcade," which
consisted of three or four wires in the form of a frame round
which were twined rose-buds mixed with lace and ribbon.

1840

IF women have never dressed so scantily as they did about
1800, they have probably never been so warmly clad
as in the 'forties. Five or six petticoats, with much solid
padding, were quite normal, and worn as they were beneath
long, full skirts, were of great advantage to the unshapely
woman, as they concealed her natural deficiencies almost
completely. But the weight of so many garments must
have been intolerable, and the crinoline, when perfected, was
a genuine reform. Shawls were still fashionable, and the
poke bonnet had begun to assume its most characteristic
shape.

Men's clothes had not yet abandoned all colour in defer-
ence to the growing fashion for black. The form of the
frock-coat gave an almost feminine appearance to the male
figure. Dress-coats also were extremely waisted. Tall hats
were very high, and more shiny than they had been previously.
Waistcoats were still elaborate and trousers very tight.

Riding became fashionable among both sexes, and the
riding-habits of the period, with tight bodices (which were
later slightly modified) and long, voluminous skirts, can be
well studied in early paintings of Queen Victoria.

1840-1845

MANTELETS, or scarf-mantelets, became almost universal. They were made of tarlatan and tulle, and were worn over " chameleon " silk dresses. Silk mantelets were trimmed with ruches of lace, guipure, or shaded ribbon of a contrasting colour.

The laced corsage was sometimes adopted for the opportunity it offered of showing the chemisette, which was either embroidered or composed of insertions of lace. Ribbons were extensively used for the decoration of the upper part of the dress. Negligés are the natural result of tight lacing, although some of the so-called negligés of the 'forties would seem stiff enough to a generation accustomed to lounge in pyjamas. Men also had their lounging clothes or smoking suits, generally of a pseudo-Turkish appearance.

Hats were shorter at the ears and more forward in front than they had previously been. Sometimes they were composed of puffings of tulle ornamented with shaded feathers.

Ball dresses had several skirts and were usually ornamented with flowers.

1845-1850

CORSAGES continued to be tight, and were made either of plain silk or of puckered taffeta. " Volans," or flounces, almost superseded all other trimmings for dresses, sometimes as many as eight being adopted, the highest reaching to within a few inches of the waist. They could be made of fringe or of puckered lace. Skirts without " volans " sometimes had a kind of stylised apron. Dresses of light materials such as *barège*, silk, muslin, or coloured tarlatan had the sleeves puckered at the wristband. Large shawls of black or white lace, or of cashmere, alternated with mantelets or *visites*—a *visite* being a kind of three-quarter-length coat with sleeves made of embroidered muslin or some similar material. Towards the end of the decade, and for cold weather, a short coat called a " Casaweck " made its appearance, made of wadded satin or velvet. Alternatives were Castilian or Andalusian cloaks made of satin, or velvet Hungarian cloaks lined with ermine, minever, or chinchilla.

Small girls' dresses were mostly made with double skirts and with fan-shaped corsages cut straight on the chest and shoulders. The bonnet for out-of-doors was very similar to that worn by their elders.

1840-1850

ALTHOUGH ball dresses were very low, and neck and shoulders bare, there was a surprising absence of neck-jewellery, a simple brooch in the front of the corsage being considered sufficient. Indeed, an attempt seems to have been made, in making the neck and shoulders the only unadorned portion of an elaborate toilette, to draw particular attention to them, and it is certainly true that in the evening dresses of the period the appearance given to the female form of emerging from complicated wrappings could be used by a clever dressmaker with most seductive effect.

Hats were composed of tulle, straw, gauze, and flowers. Open straw hats were fashionable for warm weather, and about 1846 there was a return to the eighteenth-century mode, with a hat *à la Clarissa Harlowe*, much worn at watering-places or in the country.

The beginning of the decade witnessed a great variety of male neck-wear. Some cravats were worn, as well as neck-cloths tied in a bow in front. Cravats gradually disappeared, however, and narrow ties, over which the shirt collar could be folded, were adopted by the younger men. The " dicky," or separate shirt-front, was no longer worn, being replaced by a shirt with an inset breast of finer linen. Side-whiskers, worn with a moustache and small " Imperial," were not uncommon, although they had not yet attained the extravagant dimensions of a few years later.

1850

A GENERAL levelling of the classes took place, caused partly by the new passion for travel introduced by the extension of railways ; but the novel social conditions, if they tended to make rank less important, made wealth more so, and, therefore, gave added impetus to the competition of elegance.

The main features of women's dress may be briefly summarised. Skirts were very full and often heavily flounced. The corsage was sometimes open to the waist, so as to allow the white under-garment to be seen, the two edges of the corset being kept together by ribbons or narrow strips of cloth attached by buttons. Fairly wide sleeves ending halfway down the forearm, with a sleeve of softer material appearing beneath and gathered in at the wrist, are very typical of the period. When a series of false sleeves of different lengths were worn they were called Pagodas, and were frequently white. Small over-jackets or " cannezouts " of white embroidered muslin, bordered with English lace, were much seen about 1850. The poke-bonnet was smaller than before and the top line of the head almost horizontal. Very few changes are to be noted in male dress.

1850-1855

THE dominating influence in European fashion was, since her marriage in November 1853, the Empress Eugenie. Perhaps her Spanish taste had something to do with the growing rage for violent colour, but for evening wear she added her own influence to the prevailing fashion for white. The materials used were embroidered muslin and tulle, and the panniers of dresses were enriched with ribbons of white taffeta placed at the edge to give the effect of lace. Morning dresses were of thicker stuff, such as worsted poplin. With summer costumes mantillas were worn (another sign of Spanish influence), as well as shawls of muslin or white tarlatan. For winter there was great variety of cloaks, the colours of which were dark : red, brown, and drab. Velvet was used as a trimming for everything—hats, cloaks, and dresses. Sometimes velvet was embroidered with beads, particularly coral, and sometimes it was cut to represent pansies or daisies.

Hats were of Italian straw with flowers within and without, and were furnished with a single broad ribbon of taffeta tied beneath the chin in a simple bow. Sometimes they were made of velvet and crape combined, or of velvet and silk, or of velvet and lace. Velvet, always velvet !

1855-1860

FASHION in the late 'fifties was singularly stable, and the only " decided novelty " which a contemporary record can discover is a slight increase in the size of bonnets. It was felt that the diminutive bonnet, hanging on the back of the head, was out of proportion to the mass of silk lace and other trimmings comprising a fashionable dress. An attempt was made to break the rigidity of the triangle into which woman had reduced her figure, although the method adopted—an enlargement of sleeves—had the effect of concealing the narrowness of the waist, and so intensifying the triangular effect.

Skirts were heavily flounced, and the favourite materials for ball dresses were tulle, crape, or tarlatan. Pearls, and other gems, were fashionable as trimming, being used to gather in festoons the flounces of the dress. The sleeves of a bodice of 1857 are described as terminating in bracelets of coral.

Sleeves, which were considered as articles of lingerie, were extremely elaborate, sometimes consisting of puffed muslin or tulle confined at the wrist with coloured ribbon, and enriched with five or six rows of Valenciennes lace.

Boys' dresses were more sensibly designed than formerly, but little girls were still burdened with a mass of frills and feathers borrowed from the fashions of their elders.

1850-1860

THE Paris Exhibition of 1855, which was visited in state by Queen Victoria, had the effect of confirming the dominance of French fashions and facilitating their entry into England, and in nothing was the influence of France more potent than in millinery fashions. Bonnets, which tended to be placed very far back on the head, showing the hair as far back as the crown, were small but elaborate, artificial flowers (usually roses) being the most usual decoration. For indoor wear white muslin caps were popular, worked with ribbon or embroidery, and for the country or for sunny days some curiously wide hats were designed, made of rice straw, with a deep tulle fringe depending from the brim all the way round.

For the dressing of the hair, as for the trimming of the rest of the costume, there was, particularly towards the end of the decade, a rage for pearls. Hair-nets to enclose what was called the " torsade " of hair at the back of the head, were composed of strings of pearls, and these nets were edged with pearl fringe, with tassels of pearl at the back and sides and a " cordon " of pearls passed between the bandeaux of hair in front. Two or three rows of gold chain were sometimes worn in the same fashion. Ribbon head-dresses of pink, blue, cerise, or the popular *bouton d'or* were worn at the theatre.

With evening-dress carved and inlaid fans of mother-of-pearl or ivory were fashionable. They could also be made of black or white crape, spangled with gold or silver ornaments in the Spanish style.

1860

IT was in the early 'sixties that the crinoline achieved its most astonishing proportions. Woman's form was reduced to an isosceles triangle, for even the narrowness of the waist was concealed by the width of sleeves or the amplitude of cloaks. The effect was completed by the smallness of the head-wear, with the hair confined in close-fitting bonnets tied with a bow under the chin. A pretty face was all that was needed to be irresistible, for every other portion of the female figure was most effectively concealed. In France, the hey-day of the Second Empire was a period of great luxury and ostentation. Ball dresses, especially, were costly and magnificent, and precious stones began to be worn in ever-increasing numbers. In England the influence of the Court was calculated to restrain rather than to encourage extravagance, and the death of the Prince Consort in 1861 threw a cloud over social functions, which lasted for many years. However, the reign of the crinoline was just as lasting in England as in France, and even the dresses of little girls revealed the influence of the prevailing fashion. Men's formal attire showed very little change.

1860-1865

THE " pork-pie " hat and the chignon are very characteristic of the early years of the decade.

The crinoline was sometimes worn in the street with a
skirt raised several inches from the ground, revealing ankle-
boots or miniature Hessians, a fashion much caricatured
and exaggerated in the pages of *Punch*. The drawing-up
process (if the skirts were not cut short) was effected by a
machine called the *cage américain*, an improvement on the
ordinary crinoline.

For men, the sack coat and hard round hat made their
appearance at much the same time as the famous " Dun-
dreary " whiskers. Nothing is perhaps so strange to the
modern eye as the latter, and their universality makes the
period seem more foreign than much more distant epochs.
Male attire became even more sombre than before, for the
fancy waistcoat disappeared, and was succeeded by one
made of the same material as the coat. Trousers, however,
remained strongly patterned.

Dresses, for out-of-doors, were in general simple in cut
and dark in colour, but when they were drawn up by interior
laces, they revealed brightly coloured underskirts. For
evening dresses light velvets in such colours as rose, pale
green, lilac, or turquoise were much admired. Light cloth
coats could be worn over dark dresses, and the Empress
Eugénie started a fashion for various shades of brown
foulard des Indes trimmed with black velvet.

1865-1870

THERE was a pronounced change in the shape of the
skirt about 1868. It ceased to be triangular, to
become more bottle-shaped, and by the end of the decade
was only full behind. It is possible that the origin of the
bustle is to be sought in the practice of looping up the
outer skirt. By 1868 the underskirt had, in some dresses,
become the important one, the upper skirt being caught up
almost to the hips by interior fastenings. These fastenings
were usually higher at the side than at the back, and the
general effect is not very different from that of the typical
dress of the early 'seventies. The supposition is strengthened
by the appearance of dresses in which the overskirt was not
drawn up. The back of the skirt descends in a straight,
sloping line from the waist to the ground. There is no
trace of the protuberance which was afterwards to become
so exaggerated.

Underskirts and overskirts were sometimes worn in
contrasting colours, but more frequently in different shades
of the same colour. Combinations of brown silk and bright
blue taffeta, or of green, and green and black checked taffeta,
were not uncommon. Taffeta, indeed, seemed to have replaced
velvet as the most popular material.

1860-1870

IN the early 'sixties women's hair assumed the typical chignon form, with the back hair confined in a net bag which hung from the top of the head to below the nape of the neck. Even when no net was used the form of hairdressing was very much the same, and what modifications were attempted were to be seen chiefly in evening toilettes.

In the late 'sixties the hair was dressed very flat on top, with a large bun, sometimes almost the size of the head, projecting straight back. Sometimes it was worn loose over the shoulders with very youthful effect, or else with two long curls hanging down behind, almost to the waist. The hat continued to be the smallest part of the head-dress, completely failing to cover what was still called the chignon, although its characteristic form had been abandoned. Sometimes the hair was dressed in a cascade of curls at the back of the head, echoing very closely in its complicated convolutions the shape of the back of the skirt with its incipient bustle.

Men were in general bearded, and if they shaved at all it was generally the upper lip that was left bare. Hair was worn much longer than would be thought correct to-day, and was frequently brushed forward to produce curls above the ears.

1870

THE crinoline, as we have seen, disappeared in the late 'sixties, and women's dresses assumed the bunched-up-behind appearance which they retained (with some important modifications) for twenty years. But it was not only the shape of dresses which was modified. The effect of the War of 1870–71 on France, and hence on the whole world of Fashion, was considerable. The luxury and ostentation of the Empire were felt to be out of place, and greater simplicity prevailed both in material and in ornamentation. The new mood did not last long, and accessories of the *toilette* assumed a new importance, in particular gloves, which were better made and more carefully chosen than they had ever been before. The discovery of Japanese art served to revive the interest in fans.

In men's dress a new informality was creeping in, marked by the growing success of the sack coat, the ancestor of our modern lounge suit. From having been something of an eccentricity it became very common, and but for the fact that trousers were of a different material from the coat and waistcoat, the male dress of about 1870 would seem more modern than many of the fashions that were to follow it.

1870-1875

THE corsage usually had the effect of a cavalryman's tunic, the skirts of the jacket projecting over the bustle. The draped appearance of the back of the skirt was universal, and skirts had a great many narrow flounces. Walking dresses touched the ground and some were even provided with a train. The cut of the dresses became very complicated, and a contemporary writer complains that whereas in former times an outmoded dress could still be used for something, in the 'seventies garments were composed of so many fragments of different materials that their only after-use was for the manufacture of patch-work quilts. It was the general custom to cut the dress out of two different materials, one patterned, one plain, and then to make one portion of the dress of the plain material trimmed with the patterned, and the rest of the patterned material trimmed with the plain. Check patterns were in great demand, and colours sometimes strident.

In the early 'seventies the mass of curls at the back of the head assumed, sometimes, monstrous proportions. The hair was also dressed higher at the back than it had been, with the result that the hat, which was still small, was pushed forward over the forehead.

1875-1880

ALREADY, by 1876, the bustle was much less pronounced, and that smoothness over the hips so
characteristic of the early 'eighties had begun to make its
appearance. Trimmings were elaborate, lace itself being
used, not as formerly only at the edges of garments, but
sewn onto their surface in *cascades*, *chutes*, or *ondulations*.
There were shawls, fichus, and scarves in plenty, although a
fashion writer of the period remarks that they were likely
to be draped anywhere rather than round the neck.

Dresses tended to be comparatively simple in front and
extremely complicated behind, with back fastenings (genuine
or for ornament) of knots, bows, and even of fringed tassels.

A favourite material was " faye," either for evening or
morning dresses, as it could be worked with embroidery or
combined with figured velvet. Favourite colours were
verdigris, blue marine, or pale blue, but the corsage was
sometimes constructed, in deliberate contrast, of some such
material as garnet velvet. Indian shawls were much used,
worked up into the fashionable shapes of dolman or polonaise.

1870-1880

HATS, throughout the decade, tended to be very small, and perched high on the head. They were frequently made of felt, with extremely narrow brims and high crowns. To lift the hat still farther from the head the trimming was frequently placed underneath the front brim as well as on top. Little feather toques were worn for variety, as well as hats made entirely of ribbon. The bonnet had become so reduced in size as to be distinguished from the hat, if at all, only by the ribbon tied beneath the wearer's chin.

There is usually a consonance between the general form of dress and the form of coiffure. Hair, like clothes, tended to be drawn backwards, leaving the front of the head-dress comparatively simple and falling downwards at the back in a complicated arrangement of bands and twists reminiscent of the folds and flounces at the back of the skirt. This effect was enhanced by the fashion of weaving into the hair strands of ribbon or sprays of foliage. The face was left very free, and the ears were almost always visible.

1880

THE bustle may now be said to have disappeared, although it was to appear again later. However, although the bustle had gone, dresses were still looped up behind, but lower. The back of the dress still tended to be its most elaborate part. The figure was treated as a framework on which fringed draperies could be looped and crossed, much in the fashion of the heavy window curtains of the period. Waists were very narrow, and they accentuated the apparent rigidity of the form beneath its wrappings. An attempt was made to keep the top portion of the costume very sleek, following as closely as possible the lines of the corset, and then below the hips to flare out in frills, and bows, and trimmings.

Colours were violent, plum trimmed with electric blue, or royal blue with an edging of scarlet being not uncommon. Their garishness was, however, mitigated by the almost invariable custom of wearing white lace frills at the throat and wrists. Evening-gowns were, in general, not cut so low as they had been. Men's dress had assumed its modern hue and cut.

1880-1885

THE eclipse of the bustle was very brief. Indeed, it appeared in an exaggerated form fairly early in the new decade. There was a revival of interest in the Empire period, although so-called Empire dresses bore only the most shadowy resemblance to their prototypes. The simplicity of the Empire style was entirely lacking. Extremely complicated dresses were constructed of taffeta and tulle combined, three skirts of the latter being frequently superimposed on a " sheath-skirt " of the former, or a skirt of silk was decorated with three, five, or seven "volans" of pleated tulle.

Day gowns had a certain " tailor-made " effect, especially in the bodice, which lent itself to the use of somewhat heavy materials, of which wool was the chief constituent. Hats were, in general, small, and somewhat masculine in shape, and their decoration—feathers, ribbons, or artificial flowers— was discreet. The very small bonnet tied with broad ribbons under the chin was still fashionable. The hair was worn fairly close to the head.

1885-1890

DRESSES, in the second half of the decade, were somewhat shorter, although the bustle was as pronounced as it had ever been. Bodices were not quite so masculine in cut. They followed the lines of the figure very closely, but the hard line between bodice and skirt was, in general, less noticeable. The liking for woollen materials persisted, and there was a rage of Scottish plaid patterns even in Paris. For evening toilettes for very young women it was usual to have a corsage of satin and a skirt of gauze, generally of different colours. Those who did not desire to dance wore trains. *Décolletage* was not extreme. After being eclipsed for a time by the *décolleté en cœur*, the square opening came back into favour, although for those who were afraid of being thought too thin the round opening was preferred. White gloves were, of course, *de rigueur*, and precious stones, particularly diamonds, were worn in great numbers. Hats were still sometimes worn at the theatre, but were so small as to cause little inconvenience. Hats for the street were also extremely small, although the trimming was sometimes built up to a considerable height. Hair was dressed in a small bun on the very top of the head.

The straw hat for men became very popular, not only for boating, but the silk hat held its own for ordinary wear.

1880-1890

WOMEN'S hats in this decade were, in general, small, and hair-dressing comparatively simple. A kind of compromise was evolved between the hat and the bonnet with strings, and the result grew less and less like the latter, and more and more like the former. Plumes, artificial flowers, and a blend of the two became fashionable, and complete stuffed birds were sometimes used for the trimming of hats. The hat tended to rise more and more off the head as the decade progressed, and in 1890 the front brim, which was much larger than the rest of the hat, rose steeply above the forehead. The male straw hat and felt hat were adopted by women with sporting inclinations.

Men's headgear showed a new informality. The bowler hat and the fishing cap (with brim all round) made their appearance. Vests were buttoned very high, and very little linen was exposed to view. Whiskers were no longer worn, but the moustache was almost universal.

1890

IN England, costume is inevitably modified, from time to time, in the direction of informality, by the influence of country life. The male fashions of the early nineteenth century all over Europe were the direct outcome of the Englishman's passion for riding. These fashions had gradually been formalised, and the new enthusiasm for athletics at the end of the century led to the invention of the " Norfolk jacket" and the re-discovery of knickerbockers. The complete monopoly of trousers, which had lasted since the early years of the century, was over at last.

Women's walking dresses were still cumbrous enough, and still too tight-waisted, but even in feminine attire the influence of sport was beginning to make itself felt. About 1890 also began the passion for fine underclothes, which has lasted until our own day, and was perhaps originally provoked by the plainness of the fashionable tailor-made. It seemed an added refinement to allow luxuries of dress to be almost, if not entirely, concealed beneath a plain exterior. The manufacture of extremely fine materials received an immense impetus from the new demand.

1890-1895

ONE of the distinguishing marks of the early 'nineties was the revival of the wide sleeves of 1830. Indeed, Fashion has probably never so nearly repeated itself. The silhouette of 1830 and that of 1895 are almost identical, except that in the former the skirt was considerably shorter and the waist not so narrow. Some of the hats were surprisingly similar also, although the method of hair-dressing was different. The main difference in the sleeve was that in the 'nineties only the upper arm was puffed, giving rise to the famous " leg-of-mutton " appearance so typical of the period.

Skirts were long and trailing, but were comparatively simple in cut. The " wasp-waist " had assumed its most exaggerated and pernicious form. The bodice was close-fitting, and so great was the importance attached to sleeves that even in evening-dress small puffs of ribbon were sometimes attached to the shoulders to give the fashionable effect. In the street, muffs were almost universally carried, and were small, so that they could be carried on one forearm, the other hand being perpetually occupied in lifting the dress.

1895-1900

EVENING dresses, so long as the puffed sleeve was given its due importance, could be cut very low in front, but in general bodices were designed to fit closely round the neck, and occasionally a miniature Elizabethan ruffle was added behind. A considerable quantity of often costly lace was worn, at the wrists or in the form of a frilled shirt front attached to the corsage.

Capes were fashionable throughout the decade, and their forms, echoing those of the garments, were sometimes provided with raised shoulders.

The " Norfolk jacket " for men has been already mentioned. Cycling brought in knickerbockers for women, worn with over-tunics of mannish cut, and a very small hat. Children's dresses were more sensible than they had been for some time.

The most striking innovation during the last few years of the century was the blouse—thought to have been derived from the earlier " garibaldi," a shirt-like garment which, at first, was always red, like that of the Italian general from whom it took its name. The waist was still terribly constricted, but the wasp-like effect was diminished by allowing the bodice to hang over the now universal belt.

1890-1900

BLOUSES were popular, and their fronts could be very elaborate with heavy frills of Valenciennes lace. Necks were high, and in evening-dress were sometimes encircled somewhat tightly by four or five rows of pearls or brilliants, a fashion now associated in most minds with Queen Alexandra.

About 1895 the most fashionable hat was a very small toque, to which Bird of Paradise plumes, arranged in a vertical aigrette in the centre, were an almost inevitable addition. Jet was much prized as a decoration for millinery, and it could be mingled with artificial flowers of much exaggerated size—mammoth violets or gigantic roses. Spotted veils were common, especially with the very small hats. Towards the end of the decade there was a growing tendency for hats to have wider brims and to be placed flat on the top of the head.

Men often wore a single collar, straight up all the way round, with (in evening-dress) a rather small and very flat white tie. Moustaches were still worn by almost every man, but beards had largely gone out of favour.

1900

THE end of the century is reached, but there is as yet no sign of the revolution which is to take place in women's clothes during the next twenty-five years. The corset was designed to throw the hips back and the bust forward in the most exaggerated manner possible. The lines of clothes followed those of the so-called *Art Nouveau*, with its swirling curves and its restless decorations. Even walking dresses had long trains collecting the dust of the streets at every step. The influence of sport had already produced costumes of varying degrees of usefulness, but that influence had not yet begun to affect fashionable attire.

For men of almost every position formal dress was still the usual costume, and the silk hat still reigned supreme. Indeed, the century as a whole exhibits far less striking modifications of costume than might have been expected from what was, in every respect, so revolutionary an epoch. Yet the clothes of the Nineteenth Century, viewed in retrospect, seem curiously appropriate. There is an intimate connection between costumes and manners, but no one knows exactly what it is.

14090